Didja Hear

Read aloud whimsical poems

Vincent Vinci

Silliness is a form of self entertainment,
Whether being silly by yourself or with others.

Didja Hear

All Rights Reserved © 2005 by Vincent Vinci

No part of this book may be reproduced or transmitted in any form or by any means graphic, electronic or mechanical including photocopying, recording, taping, or by any information storage retrieval system, without the permission, in writing, from the publisher.

Graphics and Layout by M&C Vinci

DoubleVee*Books

Read aloud to yourself or to a crowd.

ISBN# 978-1-4675-1034-1

Didja Hear

Read aloud whimsical poems

Vincent Vinci

DoubleVee*Books

DEER

Didja hear about the deer
That loved root beer?

His mama said,
"You oughta not drink all that soda,
It will keep you awake for goodness sake."

But the little deer just didn't care,
He continued to drink more than his fair share.

Now the little deer can't sleep and is awake all night and day,

That's what happens when you don't
Listen to what your Mama has to say.

BEAR

Didja hear about the bear
That didn't know what to wear?

He tried on many, many clothes,
none of which he chose,

Until he put on pajamas that were bright pink,
and asked his brother, "What do you think?"

"I wouldn't dare wear those pajamas anywhere."

"But Brother Bear I can't go around bare."

"Silly, you're not bare,
You've got a beautiful coat of bear hair,
That's what you should wear."

HIPPOPOTAMUS

Didja hear about the hippopotamus,
That climbed aboard a little city bus?

He was so big and fat,
That when he sat,
All the bus tires went flat.

SHEEP

Didja hear about the sheep,
That couldn't fall asleep?
No matter how hard she tried,
Her eyes remained opened wide.

"Are you still awake?" her mother asked,
"Usually you fall asleep very fast,
In fact, you fall asleep," her mother said,
"As soon as you rest your head on the bed."

"I've tossed and turned and said a prayer,
But I can't find sleep anywhere.
I tried everything to find some sleep,
I've even started counting sheep."

"We sheep don't count sheep to fall asleep,
It's people that count sheep to fall asleep'
We sheep count people to fall asleep,
So start counting people, to find your sleep."

"One people, two people, three people, four,"
It wasn't long before she started to snore.
Now she goes to sleep without a peep,
Thanks to counting people not sheep.

CHIPMUNK

Didja hear about the chipmunk
That collected a lot of junk?

Chunk-by-chunk all that junk filled his bunk.

So without a bed to rest his head,
He moved outside to sleep.

Now he's very careful what hunk of junk,
He brings home to keep.

CAT

Didja hear about the cat that chased a mouse,
All through every room of a very big house?

Until the mouse ran into a small hole in the wall,
"That's not fair," said the cat,
"I'm too tall for a hole so small."

"Aha," laughed the mouse,
"sometimes it pays to be small, after all."

PUP

Didja hear about the pup,
That never gave up?

He ran in every race,
But never won first place.

Other runners asked,
"You've lost every race you've been in,
How come you won't give in?"

"Well, you see, I have a philosophy,
With which you may or may not agree.
Someone has to lose,
So someone else can win."

"I've never won 'cause,
To me the fun is in the run."

FOX

Didja hear about the fox
That wore weird looking socks?

"Hey, little fox where did you get those wild socks?"

"I found the socks in a box, behind a bunch of rocks,"
answered the little fox.

"Are you aware you're not wearing a pair?"

"You can bet your socks I'm well aware."

"So the box didn't have a pair for you to wear?"

"I searched in there and there wasn't a pair in there."

"But your socks are all wrong, two are short, two are long,
One is green, one is black, one is red,
The fourth is blue, if I were you, I'd put them back."

"I don't care if there's no pair to wear,
'cause I just invented the Unpair.

My Unpair is going to be the style,
and everyone will wear Unpair after awhile.

With my Unpair, the catch is mix not match,
So mix a long with a short sock to make an Unpair,
one orange and one blue would be an Unpair, too,
any sort of sport sock with a dress sock,
an Unpair would do.

My Unpair will take all the lonely socks off the street,
and put them back snugly on everyone's feet.

Since we will never again have to match socks,
no one will throw away a box of Unpair socks."

FROG

Didja hear about the frog
That lived in a great big bog?
Every day he loved to play,
On a log in the middle of the bog.

If another frog came to play,
On the log in the middle of the bog,
He'd chase that frog away
From the log in the middle of the bog.
That's how he became known,
As the Hog of the Log in the Middle of the Bog.

One day a great fog covered the bog,
And the log in the middle of the bog,
That's when a bunch of frogs,
Pushed the hog frog off the log,
In the middle of the bog and into the foggy bog.

Then they climbed onto the log
in the middle of the bog,
And said to the hog frog,
"It's not fair for you not to share,
the log in the middle of the bog,
you see even us frogs don't like hogs."

KANGAROO

Didja hear about the kangaroo
That didn't know what to do?
His daddy asked, "What's wrong Hop-A-Long?"

"I lost my hop, Pop!"

"Wait a minute, stop! Stop!
Did you say you lost your hop?"

"Yes! I guess and now I'm a mess
'Cause all my hops are big flops.
Every time I try to hop my knees freeze."

"Well, I once had that problem too,
so this is what you need to do.
If you make a big sneeze," his Daddy said,
"your knees will unfreeze."

All of sudden he let out a great big Atchoo.
Thanks to his Pop he got back his hop,
And now he's a normal kangaroo.

TURTLE

Didja hear about the turtle
That hadn't come out of her shell?

All her friends thought,
She mustn't be feeling too well.

But that wasn't the case,
Why she didn't show her face.

She was too busy hanging drapes of lace,
And painting her place.

When she was done she invited everybody,
To a big Redecorating-Celebration Party.

CROCODILE

Didja hear about the crocodile
That never sheds a tear?

He's the only crocodile
That always smiles from ear to ear.

All his friends asked, "You never shed crocodile tears,
can you tell us why?"

"It's very simple" he answered with a sigh,
"it's 'cause I hate to cry."

GOAT

Didja hear about the goat,
That ate his master's hat and coat?
Crunch, crunch, munch, munch,
"This hat sure is a delicious lunch,
I wish I had hats by the bunch,
Then I'd eat one every day for lunch.

Soon my master will be looking for his hat,
'Cause he doesn't know where the hat's at,
But you and I know where it's at,
And we're sure not going to tell him that.

He'll look around and around,
But the hat won't ever be found,
And the coat too is nowhere in sight,
'Cause I ate the coat for supper last night.

I ate the whole coat, the collar, pockets and sleeves too,
But not the zipper and buttons 'cause,
They're too hard to chew,
Of all the pieces, the sleeves tasted the best,
Still I enjoyed every bit of the rest.

There are many goats that prefer people's hats and coats,
Than munching on a big barrel full of oats,
So listen to this whiskered old goat,
Be very careful where you leave your hat and coat."

GIRAFFE

Didja hear about the giraffe
That had a very unusual laugh?

His neck was so long, that when he laughed,
It came out as a song.

All the animals shouted, "Laugh, laugh Giraffe!
So we can sing along with your song."

Before long the group was the rage,
And appeared on every animal stage.
They'll soon be on your TV,
Just you wait and see.

If you don't believe this is true,
Please go to your nearest zoo,

And ask for the Giraffe,
With the unusual laugh.

DINOSAUR

Didja hear about the dinosaur
That didn't want to roar anymore?
"Why don't you want to roar anymore?
You used to love to roar before."

"I did adore a good roar before, but now I think more and more,
that roaring is very boring, and not as enjoyable as snoring.

What's a big roar good for anyway? It just scares other animals away,
but I'd rather have them stay, so we can become friends that way."

"But you're a dinosaur, you're supposed to roar,
it's Mother Nature's Law, all dinosaurs must roar.
Besides your roar is so loud, it can scare away a whole crowd,
you should be very proud, you have a roar that loud."

"If you think I have a real loud roar,
you should hear me snore,
Last night, with one big snore, I tore off my bedroom door
And blew my brother out of bed, and onto the floor.

With my new big loud snore,
I can ignore Mother Nature's Law,
And have more fun than before,
That's why I don't like to roar anymore."

RHINO

Didja hear about the rhino,
That didn't know,
Where she wanted to go?

"I think I'll go to the movie show,
But then maybe I won't go to the movie show,
Maybe I'll go to the baseball game.

But if I go to the baseball game,
I'll miss the movie show,
And that would be a shame.

Maybe I'll go visit my friend Fred,
Oops, it's too early to see Fred,
'Cause Fred is a sleepy head,
And is probably still in bed.

Maybe I'll just go for a ride on my bike,
But then again maybe I should go for a hike,
Then I wouldn't need to take a bike,
If I went for a hike.

But then again maybe I should go to the store,
But what would I go to the store for?
I have everything I need and maybe more,
Then I'll skip going to the store.

I can always go to the park,
But if I go to the park,
I better go before it gets dark,
'Cause you can't see anything when it's dark in the park.

Maybe I'll stay home and watch TV.
There's lots of programs on TV,

So which programs should I see?
'Cause too much TV isn't good for me.

I still don't know where I want to go,
I'd better make up my mind very soon,

'Cause it's already half past noon.
I guess I'll go someplace I don't know.

To do that I'll just go out and about,
You know just walking here and there,
That may lead me nowhere or maybe somewhere,
But at least I'll be getting some fresh air."

HORSE

Did you hear about the little horse that was lost?

"I lost my way," he told the policeman, "when I wandered off to play."

"That's okay, I know the way so I'll get you home today.

"But first I have important advice," the policeman said,
"listen carefully 'cause I won't say it twice.

When you go out to play, don't ever roam,
always stay close to home."

GNU

Didja hear about the Gnu,
That ran away from the zoo?
Why he ran away from the zoo,
Nobody in the zoo knew.

Not even the zookeeper knew,
Why the Gnu ran away from the zoo,
And the animal trainers too,
Along with the rest of the zoo crew,
Wondered why the Gnu ran away from the zoo.

So the zookeeper called together the zoo crew,
He then told everyone exactly what he knew,
About the Gnu that ran away from the zoo,
And what he wanted each zoo crew member to do.

"This is different than,
The time the moose got loose,
Or when the goose left her roost.

It's worse than when the goat,
Ate her trainer's hat and coat,
Or when the horse became hoarse.

This is extremely serious,
And mighty mysterious, too.
So to find out why the Gnu,
Chose to run away from our zoo,
This is what we're going to do.

Go ask every animal and bird too,
If they have the tiniest clue,
Why the Gnu ran away from the zoo.
And I'll call every zookeeper,
I know from here to Timbuktu,

To see if they've had a Gnu,
That ran away from their zoo."

When the zoo crew was through,
Asking everyone in the zoo,
About the runaway Gnu,

Most of them said they had no clue.
But here's a few that thought they knew.

"I'll bet it was the full moon," said the big Baboon,
"He must have been daffy in the head," the Lion said,
"Maybe the Gnu had the flu," said the Cockatoo,
"Isn't he the one called Wildebeest?" asked the Caribou,
"I think he went to buy new shoes and socks," guessed the Fox.

Then the zookeeper told the zoo crew,
"Every zookeeper I talked to,
Said they never had a Gnu,
run away from their zoo.

"So as far as I can see, we still have a mystery,
Now what can we do?" the zookeeper started asking the zoo crew,

When all of the sudden out of the blue,
The Gnu came walking back into the zoo.

"Well! How do you do!" said the zoo crew to the Gnu,
"And where were you and why did you run away from our zoo?"

"'Cause everyone, even the children, call me a Wildebeest,
But I'm not wild in the least, so why do they
Call me a Wildebeest?"

"It's a shame you don't like your name,
But we have another name for you,"
The zookeeper told the Gnu.

"A Wildebeest's other name is Gnu,
In fact there's a song about you,
"I'm a Gnu the g-nicest work
Of g-nature in the zoo."

"Goodbye Wildebeest I'm through with you,
From now on everybody calls me a Gnu."

OTHER BOOKS
By
Vincent Vinci

A Single Raindrop

Toto's Music

Allison Visits Her Bird Friends

CPSIA information can be obtained
at www.ICGtesting.com
Printed in the USA
LVIC06n1517070414
380668LV00010B/95